DATE DUE

SEQUOYAH

By C. W. Campbell

DILLON PRESS, INC.
MINNEAPOLIS, MINNESOTA

© 1973 by Dillon Press, Inc. All rights reserved

Dillon Press, Inc., 500 South Third Street
Minneapolis, Minnesota 55415

Printed in the United States of America

Library of Congress Cataloging in Publication Data

Campbell, Chester W.
　Sequoyah.

　(The Story of an American Indian)
　SUMMARY: A biography of Sequoyah, inventor of a writing system for the Cherokee language.
　1. Sequoyah, 1770?-1843—Juvenile literature.
[1. Sequoyah, 1770?-1843. 2. Cherokee Indians—Biography]
E99.C5S382　　　970.3 [B]　　　72-91159
ISBN 0-87518-057-4

SEQUOYAH

Sequoyah was born in the Cherokee village of Tuskegee, Tennessee around 1770. Called The Lame One because he walked with a limp, Sequoyah became a blacksmith and silversmith. Then he enlisted in the War of 1812, and as he observed the white soldiers reading and writing letters home, he became obsessed with their "talking leaves." Determined to create a writing system for the Cherokee language, he persisted through many attempts and failures before he finally evolved the 86-character syllabary that does, indeed, capture the Cherokee language in "talking leaves." His accomplishment has assured Sequoyah a place in the history of man's great achievements.

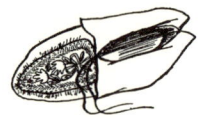

Contents

I   HIS FATHER'S SHADOW   page 1

II   A STORY TO REMEMBER   page 10

III   SILVERSMITH, BLACKSMITH   page 20

IV   BEGINNING OF A MIRACLE   page 29

V   A DREAM COME TRUE   page 43

VI   THE LAST FAREWELL   page 57

CHAPTER I

His Father's Shadow

From the very beginning something set Sequoyah apart from the other Indian boys in the village, but it was not entirely because his father had been white. Having a white father was in itself no disgrace among the Cherokees. Many Indian women had married white men long before Wut-teh, Sequoyah's mother, had married the white man called Gist.

This custom was one of the many changes that had come to the Cherokees since the arrival of the white men. Two centuries earlier, when the Cherokees were first discovered by the Spanish explorer de Soto in 1540, they lived in towns and villages in the vast mountainous region of the southern Appalachians in what is today southern Virginia, western North and South Carolina, eastern Tennessee, northern Georgia, and northeastern Alabama. Their hunting range covered more than forty thousand square miles, and they numbered as many as twenty-five thousand. The Cherokees were the most powerful nation in the east. Had they been wise enough to band together they might have held the advancing white man to the level coast land.

But the Cherokees did not realize the danger then.

Although their ancestors, the Tallegewi, had been fierce and warlike, the Cherokees offered de Soto and his party hospitality and friendship. De Soto did not stay long and when he left, he repaid their kindness by taking with him gold and silver and other convincing evidence that the Cherokee country offered riches beyond belief. And land — there was lots of land!

And so the white men came: first the Spaniards, then the British, the French, and the Germans. With them came the changes that were to alter the Indians' way of life forever.

To the Indians, gold and silver were only for making jewelry. To the white man, however, gold was very valuable and something to be desired. Cherokees cared nothing for material things. To them, a friend was a friend regardless of what he owned. But the white man thought that some men were better than others because of what they possessed. The white men were convinced, too, that their way was the right way. They brought their own laws to replace those of the Indians, and their guns soon replaced bows and arrows.

True, the changes had been slow. Nevertheless, by the time Sequoyah was born, around 1770, the changes could be felt. One of the first things to be changed was the Indians' source of food. The buffalo had long since been driven westward, and now deer were slowly being killed or pushed farther back into the deep ravines between the mountains. It had become harder and harder for the Indians to find suitable patches of upland soil large enough to plant their cornfields. Even the smaller fields where beans and squash could grow were becoming

3 HIS FATHER'S SHADOW

scarce. Thus it was only a matter of time before many Cherokees gave up farming and turned to raising the white man's sheep, chicken, cattle, and hogs.

Still, the Cherokees tried to get along. They continued to accept and treat well the traders and hunters who came into Cherokee country from the north. These white men brought needles, knives, and scissors wrapped in bright cloth and colorful ribbons; they brought shiny brass and bronze kettles of all sizes to trade for furs.

This was how Wut-teh, Sequoyah's mother, met his father. The man called Gist first met Wut-teh on one of his trips to the Cherokee village of Tuskegee, near Fort Loudon on the Little Tennessee River in Tennessee, in an area called the Overhill Cherokee country. A few weeks later he traded a few trinkets for her, and they were married. As was the Cherokee custom, Wut-teh built their house a little apart from the tribal village,

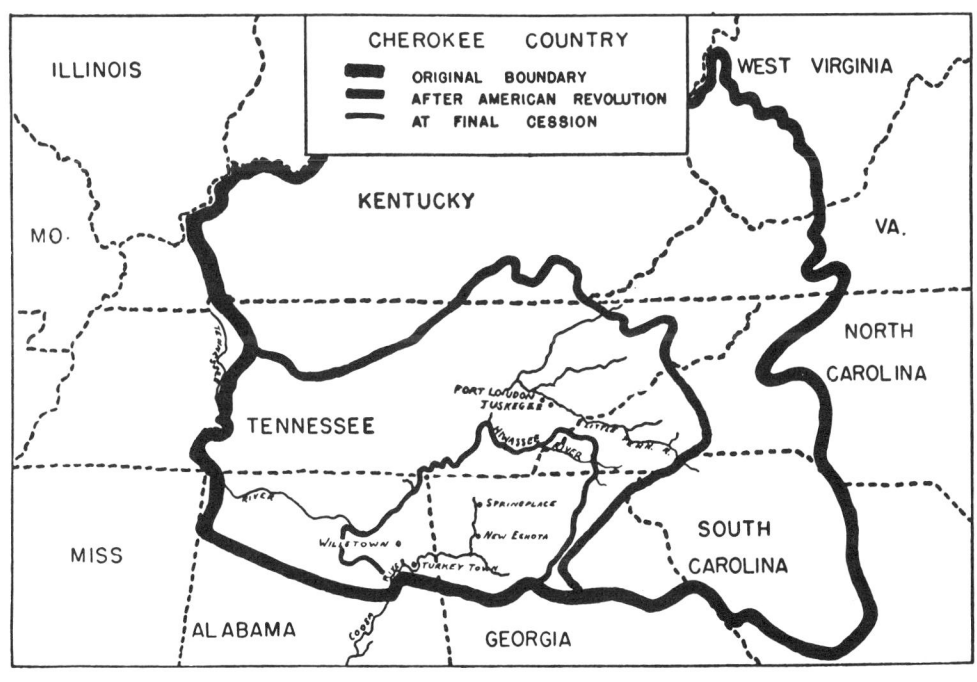

furnished it, grew the crops, waited upon her husband, and did everything possible to make his new life satisfying and full of contentment. But before too many moons had passed, the man rode off on a trading mission. Sequoyah was never to see his father. Although Wut-teh waited for her husband's return, he never came back. The man called Gist had returned to his own world, leaving Wut-teh alone to raise and care for her son the best way she could.

But that was no disgrace. In those days marriage by tribal law, under which Wut-teh and Sequoyah's father were married, was an established practice on the frontier. Often such marriages were happy ones, and many of them lasted as long as the couples lived. On the other hand, if the marriage did not work out well, the couple did not quarrel; the man simply said good-bye and went away, leaving his cabin, his corn patch, and his livestock to his wife and children.

So Sequoyah was not alone in not having a father. Other Cherokee children had managed without a father for a while, and perhaps Sequoyah should have been able to, also. But there was still something else that made Sequoyah different from the other boys: he was lame. It is not known how or when Sequoyah became lame. Some have said he was born that way; others, that his crippled leg was caused by a hunting accident. But from the earliest accounts of Sequoyah's life, it was said that he walked with a limp. If ever a Cherokee boy needed a father to teach him things, it was Sequoyah.

The Cherokees were devoted to their children. Never was a Cherokee father so busy that he could not take time to teach his sons the way of the hunter. Never was he so busy that he could not take time to construct little bows and arrows with which a boy could hunt rabbits, or to make small blow guns to shoot crickets with.

Cherokee women knew that all boys needed a father, and usually they remarried. Wut-teh never remarried, and so Sequoyah never had even a stepfather, or any brothers or sisters.

Sequoyah did have two uncles, both of whom were respected men in the tribal council. But a boy must not burden the wise men of the council with foolish things such as how to track deer or how to tan a hide. No, Sequoyah knew better than that. A Cherokee was taught from early childhood to respect his elders. Only when spoken to was a youngster allowed to speak. Sequoyah decided that he would have to learn what he could from his mother. What she could not tell him, he would just have to find out the best way he knew how.

That is probably what set Sequoyah to wondering about his father. He was curious. What had his father been like? Had he been one of the few good white men he had heard others speak about, who came in friendship to teach and to help the Cherokee toward a better life? Or had he been like the many other white men who came with greed in their pale eyes? Sequoyah wanted to know.

He went several times to Wut-teh to ask her about his father. Each time she would smile and say simply that he should not worry himself about it. But Sequoyah wanted to know, and he was determined to seek further. He went to other Cherokees and asked, "Did you know the white man who was my father?"

He got few answers. Because Wut-teh had built her house away from the tribal village, many had seen her white husband only a few times, so they did not know. Still others told him it made no difference who his father was; he had been a white man and that was that. Was it not the white men who had brought the Cherokees the dread disease called smallpox, they reminded him. The boy nodded; this was something he knew about.

There had been a smallpox epidemic in the village before Sequoyah was born, and the results could still be seen. Smallpox had first come to the Cherokees in the 1700s. Besides the many deaths the disease caused, it so disfigured survivors that many warriors, after seeing their pitted and scarred faces reflected in the clear streams, committed suicide. And this, according to Cherokee beliefs, was the worst thing an Indian could do. Never could he be at peace in the land of the great beyond. Instead, he was destined to wander forever in search of Yo-he-Wah ("The Great Spirit"), for Yo-he-Wah alone could grant forgiveness.

Twice the smallpox had taken its toll of the Cherokees. One of Sequoyah's uncles, Tal-tsu'ika ("Two Heads") had been stricken with the disease. Only through the grace of Yo-he-Wah had he survived. Even so, the smallpox left his once handsome face so ugly and scarred that he refused ever to look at himself again.

Yes, Sequoyah knew all too well about the white men's sickness. They had brought other sickness too, such as mumps, whooping cough, tuberculosis — even the common cold. Such illnesses were strange to the Cherokees. Even though the medicine men had tried every cure and magic formula they knew, many had died.

Why then did Sequoyah want to know this white man? Sequoyah and Wut-teh were probably better off without him anyway, they said. To this the lonely boy merely shrugged and limped away. That was not the answer he wanted. Someone must have known his father. But who? Then it came to him — Old Kaluna would know!

Old Kaluna had seen many things and had learned much in his long life. Once his wisdom had been much sought after by the other men on the council. Now he was looked upon as a conjuror, one who casts spells. They no longer needed or heeded his words. So he spent his hours dreaming of the old days and telling the legends and history of the Cherokee people to the youngsters. Surely, Old Kaluna would know. He was wise in many things.

When Sequoyah went to Old Kaluna, he was told, "The man you speak about was no good. He was *Unaka* ("white"), and all white men's words are smooth as water that covers jagged rocks beneath. When your father went away, Wut-teh was sad. Then Yo-he-Wah gave you to her and she was glad. That is all you need to know."

The boy was stubborn and persisted until Old Kaluna said finally, "You are young yet and do not understand. It matters not who your father was. What matters is who you are and what you become. Your ways are not those of the Unakas, you are Cherokee, and one of Yo-he-Wah's *Ani-Yun-Wiya* ("Principal People"). We are the true descendants of the Tallegewi. For this you must be proud, because you are Cherokee. But I will tell you this. I know only that your father's last name was Gist.

His first name I do not know. I know also that there were two white men called Gist in our village. Which of these was your father, I do not know. Only Wut-teh knows. That is for her to say."

Sequoyah went again to Wut-teh and told her what he had learned. Wut-teh showed no surprise at her son's repeated question, or at his new knowledge. In a way, she was glad he was so determined. It showed he had persistence, a good Indian trait. For that, she was grateful. Nevertheless, she was Indian too, and she would not tell him just yet. In time maybe she would, but not now. So Wut-teh's answer was as before. Then, she sent him out to gather firewood and search for the different herbs and plants that she often used in preparing her meals.

Sequoyah was to wonder about his father many times in his early life. He was not alone in his puzzlement, for today, some two hundred years later, the mystery surrounding the identity of his father still exists.

Some say his father was a man named Nathaniel Gist of Baltimore, Maryland. Nathaniel Gist, a hunter, trader, and explorer who was on the friendliest of terms with the Indians, was said to have been living in the Tuskegee village shortly before Sequoyah's birth.

Others say that his father must have been a wandering German trader whose name was George Gist, who was also known to have lived in Tuskegee. George Gist was not related to Nathaniel and it is doubtful that they even knew one another. Two more different men can hardly be imagined. Nathaniel was an honorable man of good family; George was known to both Indians and whites as a cheat and a liar. By the time he left the Indian town of Tuskegee, the Cherokees had already started calling him *A-sga'-si-ti-,* which means "ugly" or "mean." The true Cherokee language contained no profanity, and this was their worst term of abuse.

George Gist never stayed in any one place very long, and shortly after Sequoyah's birth he disappeared. It was later reported that he had been killed in another village to the north. There were other reports too, telling of his misdeeds and his death, but they are hard to prove.

One reason why many people believe that George Gist was his father is the fact that Sequoyah's white name was also George Gist. It was a common practice among the Cherokee women to give their half-breed sons their father's name. Since Wut-teh chose George as her son's white name instead of Nathaniel it seems logical to say that George Gist was the father of Sequoyah. Of course, no one can know for certain if this is true. In any case, Sequoyah never knew why Wut-teh refused to answer his questions about his father, for she died years later without ever telling him.

Even so, the boy seemed to sense that his father may not have been the best sort of person. He made up his mind that he was going to get rid of the shadow that lay over him because of his mysterious white father, even if it took him all his life.

Sequoyah could not know that because of his determination he would someday become one of the most remarkable men ever to emerge in the history of the American Indian. His is one of the most inspiring stories of a man's fight to overcome ignorance.

CHAPTER II

A Story to Remember

The white name which his mother had given him did not make him white, Sequoyah told himself fiercely. Never would he be white and never would he learn the white man's language. He was Cherokee, and of the Red Paint Clan.

That was Wut-teh's clan too, because Cherokee children belonged to their mother's clans and families, whether their fathers were Indian or not. For that reason Sequoyah should have had a real and recognized place in the tribe. Yet there were some things a lame boy could not do successfully, no matter how hard he tried.

At first he had played the other boys' games. Season after season he ran in the foot races. And though he was always the first to make ready, he usually ended up watching longingly after the others as they ran swiftly and surely the full distance and then back again.

The ceremonial ball games had been no different. Playing ball was a serious matter for young Indians. In earlier days the Cherokees had thought of the ball games as a preparation for war. For that reason there was much honor involved in playing the games, and often there were bets on the outcome.

11 A STORY TO REMEMBER

All day the lame boy ran back and forth, up and down the field, trying to follow the ball and its movements. Once he even tried to block the Red players when his own side had the ball, but in his haste he stumbled and fell, causing the Red players to win. Everyone had laughed at him then. Some of the men watching let him know that he had lost the game for the Black side. One warrior told the boy that he had cost him his best set of arrows and two knives.

Sequoyah would never make a warrior, they said. If he could not last a whole day in running and jumping, how could he ever expect to last a whole day in battle? No, it would be better for him if he would not try to be something he was not.

Losing did not bother the lame boy as much as the fact that he had failed to prove himself a Cherokee. He wanted so much to prove that he was as much Indian as they were. Again and again he tried, but always it was the same. Either he was blamed for losing an important game, or he was laughed at because he finished last. After a while the boy stopped playing the games, kept to himself, and took long walks in the woods surrounding the village.

One day he was sitting under a clump of mountain laurel when Old Kaluna came up to him and said, "I have been watching Sequoyah and he is sad because he always loses. But there are other things which are more important, things that do not require him to run fast."

Like Sequoyah and Wut-teh, Old Kaluna was of the Red Paint Clan. And from the Red Paint Clan came the medicine men, the casters of spells. Old Kaluna was old and did not do much magic anymore; even so, he was still wise in many things. Sequoyah had always liked Old Kaluna. Now, he felt drawn to him. It was as though the old man's soft words had hypnotized him.

"There is something you must know, and you must remember it all, for it concerns you. It is a story about the Tallegewis."

No doubt Sequoyah had heard the story before, when he had been younger, and with the others. This day, however, the words were meant especially for him. He did not know it then, but he would remember the story many times in the course of his life. Over sixty years later it would start him on an adventure from which he would never return.

Old Kaluna began: "Long ago, all Cherokees lived in cliffs and caves in a place called Mexico. They were as many as all the trees in the forests. When a great famine came upon the land, they became like frightened *tsi-tus* ("rabbits"), and knew not what to do. But there was one who was wise and not afraid. He prayed to Yo-he-Wah to make the Cherokees a new land where there would be plenty for all.

"Yo-he-Wah made the land and while it was yet flat, soft, and wet, he sent Sali the great buzzard and grandfather of all buzzards to fly over the new earth. When Sali came to the country that was to belong to the Cherokee he became tired and his flapping wings touched the ground. Where the wings struck the earth, there was a valley. Where they turned up again there was a mountain. That is how the land that the Cherokees love so much was formed.

The Great Smoky Mountains, where Sequoyah grew up

"When the Cherokees began their journey to this new land, it was the time of year when the Thunder Man and the Lightning roamed the hills, flashing and grumbling. But they never struck a Cherokee, for there was one among them who had befriended the Thunder Man. In return, the Thunder Man kept them from perishing that winter by sending his friend, the Lightning, to place their first fire in the hollow stump of a sycamore tree."

Old Kaluna sat down. He had finished the story.

This, Sequoyah did not understand. "What does the story have to do with me?" he asked.

"You are foolish," said Old Kaluna. "Games will not make you a man. Wisdom and courage will. Look! I tell you this. It was a medicine man of the Red Paint Clan who gave Sali strong wings to fly over the earth. It was a medicine man of the Red Paint Clan who befriended the Thunder Man. Always it has been the Red Paint Clan who helped in time of trouble. It will always be this way.

"Now, I tell you this. The time is coming when the Cherokees will need a great leader to follow. Already the white man is at the door of the Cherokee. There is no place left to go that the white man will not come.

"The Cherokee must learn the secret of the white man's strength. It is not his *galo-gwa* ("gun") that makes his strong medicine. No! I tell you this. The white man can make strong medicine without his gun. His secret is more powerful than the gun. Someday a Cherokee will learn the secret. Then he will be great and the Cherokees who are the Principal People will be great, for they too will have the strong medicine of the white man. Only a medicine man can do this.

"Sequoyah is foolish. He worries too much about a game instead of trying to gain wisdom early. It is better that Sequoyah learn the ways of the medicine men than to play the games of foolish children. If Sequoyah wants to be great, I will teach him what I know. I will tell him all the stories of the Tallegewis. Other medicine men will also teach and tell what they know."

And so the lonely boy joined the wanderings of the medicine men. When they went out seeking herbs and plants and the sacred bloodroot, the lame boy went too. A few times he was taken to where the rarest plants grew. Before long he knew the name of every plant and how it could be used.

He learned, too, that no one medicine man knew everything; instead, each one had special ways of his own which the boy quickly learned. And with his keen memory he learned all of their formulas for spells, even the most secret ones.

If Sequoyah thought this would make the other boys accept him, he was sadly mistaken, because it only gave them more reason to mock him and call him names. They were not afraid of the half-breed, they taunted. After all, he was too young to put a spell on them.

This did not seem to bother Sequoyah. He knew they had never really accepted him anyway. What he did not know, however, was whether it was because of his white blood or because he was lame.

For a long time he had held the belief that somewhere he would find a plant which would help Old Kaluna cure his lame leg. Wut-teh, too, longed to bring her son normal strength, so she paid the old medicine man four earthen jars filled with parched corn, four deerskins, and four pair of moccasins trimmed in bright beads to work his magic spell.

Old Kaluna agreed to try. He motioned for Sequoyah to follow him on a trail into the woods until they came to an old tree that was gnarled and twisted from being struck by lightning many years before. A tree such as this was sacred; there was great magic in the bark of a tree that refused to be defeated. It stood alone, yet its twisted form protected many other trees. That, said Old Kaluna, was a good lesson for Sequoyah.

Then, walking around the tree from right to left four times, the medicine man removed a piece of bark with great care and placed it inside his robe. He and the boy then went back to the village.

Among the Cherokees, four was a sacred number, and much depended on doing things in four. Thus, for four days and four nights the boy lay on the floor in Old Kaluna's house, surrounded by hot stones over which the old medicine man poured water to make steam.

Four times Old Kaluna rubbed Sequoyah's crippled leg with the bark of the twisted tree. This would give his leg strength and courage to grow straight, the old man said. Four times he blew a mixture of sourwood bark and ginseng root over the boy. Then Old Kaluna took a comb of bone made of four sharp splinters from a turkey leg and raked it across the boy's naked leg. Four times he did that, and four times the youth bit his lip, although no sound escaped. Once he passed out from the pain, but never did he break silence. He was Cherokee. Cherokees did not cry at pain.

Old Kaluna tried other things too in those four days. At the end of the fourth night Sequoyah was too weak to walk and Old Kaluna had to carry him to the river, where he lowered the boy into the water. He stayed there four hours before Old Kaluna told him it was time to come out.

Many Cherokees had been cured by going to the river. Not so Sequoyah. In the end he was still lame. Old Kaluna said he had sung and prayed that Sequoyah might become a fine man, worthy in every way to be a Cherokee and a leader. He had treated Wut-teh's son as best he knew, but Yo-he-Wah had not made it possible for him to put more life into Sequoyah's shortened leg. He would be crippled for life.

Little by little as Sequoyah grew older, Wut-teh took him from his wanderings with the medicine men and taught him new wisdom with which to occupy his mind. In the short time the white trader had been her husband, she had learned the value of furs in white man's money. She knew the proper weight of silver in her hand, and the ring of good and bad coins. These things she taught to her son.

Along with her other farming activities Wut-teh now had some cows to tend, and Sequoyah, despite the fact it was women's work, helped with their care. Quite often he would go with Wut-teh and the other Cherokee women when they went to gather herbs in the hills, greens by the water, and wild muscadine grapes in the mountains. In late fall they would set carefully tended fires to clear away the underbrush in the chestnut groves to make the nuts easier to gather. Years later it was to become a legend among the people in the Great Smoky Mountains that Indian summer, with its soft smoky haze and gentle warmth, was created by these autumn fires.

When he was not on a trading mission with Wut-teh or helping her with some farming chore, he would go off into the forest where he would think and dream of being a great leader. Sitting cross-legged on a rock beside a mountain stream that tumbled and churned its way over boulders, the boy would listen to the sounds of the animals and birds busy in the forest around him.

He knew the call of the katydid in the late summer, when its cry signaled that the corn was ripe enough to eat. He knew the song of the chickadee and the redbird. He knew the snort of the deer, the bark of the fox, and the insistent chatter of the squirrel.

He knew the call of the sparrow too, for once that had been his name. On the day of his birth a sparrow had perched in the window of Wut-teh's house and sounded its approval that her baby had been born a boy. It had been a good sign, so Wut-teh gave her son the Indian name of *Tsis-kwa'ya* ("The Sparrow"). It was only later, when other Cherokees began to notice his lameness, that they began calling him Sequoyah, "The Lame One."

That was all right with Sequoyah. Let them call him what they wanted. Names did not hurt him. Someday, he promised himself, his life would be one that not only the Cherokees, but all Indians and whites as well, would never forget. How he would do this, he did not yet know, but he felt sure that he would find a way.

Sequoyah sat quietly for a long time listening to the

many different sounds in the forest. Absentmindedly he picked up a small colored piece of slate rock and began to draw designs with it on the large boulder he was sitting on. With his quick eye, he caught a glimpse of a tiny ground squirrel holding an acorn in its front paws. Without any effort at all he drew its picture on the big rock. The boy was amazed!

Was that a squirrel he had drawn? It certainly looked like a squirrel. Yes, Sequoyah decided, even though the crack in the rock kept it from being a perfect likeness, one could still see it was a squirrel.

For the first time in a long while the boy felt a sense of pleasure within himself. He had sone something by himself, without any help from anyone. It was a good feeling. He could draw.

The young boy spent many hours after that in the woods and hills around his home drawing simple pictures of animals, flowers, and many other things. His sketches were rough-looking, mostly because he had not yet learned of the thin, flimsy white material called paper.

For hours on end he drew his pictures on bark taken from sycamore trees, using pieces of charred wood from the fireplace. He drew pictures in the dirt. He drew pictures on other rocks. And with a small knife that Wut-teh had given him he carved pictures on the board fence that surrounded the livestock.

Sequoyah was about fifteen then, and finding out he could draw had been a fascinating discovery for the lonely boy. More important, he was soon to find out he could do other things with his hands.

CHAPTER III

Silversmith, Blacksmith

For centuries the Cherokees had worked in wood, clay, shell, silver, and semi-precious stones. On occasion, when they could obtain copper from their northern kinsmen the Iroquois, the Cherokees had also learned to hammer the copper into jewelry for themselves and their families. Many of the Indian women made fine pottery. Others were skillful at the white man's loom and could weave cloth made of hemp or milkweed fiber. In everything they did, the Cherokees were fine workers and craftsmen.

In his desire to be a good Cherokee, Sequoyah was glad to prove his skill by making utensils like those he saw in use at the white settlements. The lame youth learned how to use the saw and hammer, and built a good springhouse, a small building used to keep food cool, which delighted Wut-teh.

When he was sixteen, Sequoyah made a chair and sewing table for Wut-teh. The next year, at seventeen, Sequoyah built her a loom room, working singlehandedly until the roof was on and the floor laid. Then he set about to build her a new loom, strong and fine enough to weave cotton for shirts and aprons.

During this time, Sequoyah's interest in drawing had increased and at the age of eighteen he turned to painting. Although he had never heard of camel hair brushes, the youth discovered for himself that the hair of wild animals made fine brushes.

To add color to his paintings he ground berries and roots and continually experimented in mixing them. Still unfamiliar with paper, Sequoyah painted his pictures on sycamore bark and corn husks. His horse and deer paintings were particularly successful. And even though he had never seen one, it was said that no one could paint a better buffalo than The Lame One.

The boy delighted in watching the faces of others when they looked at his colorful drawings. No doubt it was this pleasure that inspired him to start working in silver.

By this time Wut-teh had increased her trading business to other villages and white settlements. Sequoyah, in helping her, broadened his own contacts outside the tribe, though he still refused to learn the white man's language.

Nevertheless, his hands seemed to shape themselves naturally around any tool he touched, and before long some of the things he made could be sold for coined money. From these coins he learned to make his first silver ornaments. These he also sold. And when he made his next trading trip for Wut-teh, it was not only for fur and trade items that he went. It was to seek out the silversmiths.

From one he bought a hammer and from another a bit of sharpened steel. Hurrying home, he built a slow fire on a stone and melted some of the silver coins in a metal bowl. From this silver he made bracelets, earrings, and buttons. From other melted silver he made buckles, breastplates, armbands, silver knife handles, spurs, and even a silver snuff box for the chief.

At first, he made only plain ornaments. But as his skill improved he began to experiment and put designs of animals and birds on his silver pieces. Then he rubbed them with wood ash and a piece of buckskin until they glowed. His unending patience and attention to detail showed in the unusually fine work he did. Sequoyah was soon in much demand as a silversmith, both by the Cherokees and by the few whites who knew him.

Sequoyah was about twenty then, and his ability to work with silver and draw had helped him to gain a little recognition among his tribesmen. He had acquired a few friends.

As his silver trade increased, one of his new friends advised him to begin using a trademark. Sequoyah did not quite know what this meant. The friend explained that it meant putting his name or mark on everything he made, so that the one who made it would be known forever.

That seemed like a good idea to the silversmith. How did one go about obtaining such a trademark, he wanted to know?

The friend sent him to another man who agreed to set the letters of the trademark in print for him. When asked what name he wanted printed, Sequoyah thought for a long time.

He was Cherokee. He was also half white, and there

was no way around that. Nearly all the half-breeds he knew used their white names on important and official matters. Some, in fact, had begun to use them at the council talks.

Sequoyah reasoned that his silver work was important. And was it not true that more and more whites were buying his wares? It was important, then, that they know the silver work was his; so Sequoyah told the man to print the letters for the name George Gist.

After laboring over the task for sometime, the man managed to spell it Guess instead of Gist. Sequoyah was satisfied, and he sunk the letters in a steel punch, thereafter stamping all his silver pieces with that name. This is why Sequoyah has become known by two different white names, George Guess as well as George Gist.

Shortly after Sequoyah turned twenty-one, Wut-teh died. The Lame One was deeply saddened. Wut-teh had been more than a mother; she had been a friend. She had understood her son, and as long as she was alive he had not been alone.

For a long time, the crippled youth had been thinking about leaving the Tuskegee village. Now that Wut-teh was gone, there was nothing to keep him there any longer. The few friends he had now could not make him forget the loneliness and frustration he had felt while growing up.

Within a few days Sequoyah had settled his affairs. He traded what he could for more silver, took what he needed to begin his new life, and gave the rest away. Then, turning his back on his hometown in the Overhill Cherokee country, he headed south for the valley towns.

Sequoyah evidently wandered aimlessly the next two years, for artistic silver work bearing his trademark showed up in many of the Indian towns and white settlements throughout what is now North and South Carolina, Alabama, and Georgia.

By the time Sequoyah reached Willstown, Alabama, he was not only a superb silver craftsman but had begun to show an interest in blacksmithing, which he had learned by watching the white smiths in the settlements.

Willstown was a much larger settlement than Sequoyah had ever seen. For one thing, there were more white people. For another thing, travel here followed the streams and rivers. The Tennessee River was busy with boat traffic, and trails also wound along beside the river. There were houses with separate rooms for cooking and sitting. In Willstown more people had horses and wagons than in Tuskegee. Some even had closed-in wagons called carriages.

With all the activity going on, Sequoyah realized that Willstown would be an ideal place to begin a new life and a new trade. He decided to build his house in the Cherokee village which was a few miles from Willstown on the banks of the Coosa River. He quickly found out that there were many other Cherokees from Tuskegee in the village. Some he did not know very well. Others he remembered from the way they treated him as a boy.

To Sequoyah it seemed almost funny. He had left the Overhill country to escape bad memories and start a new life, and now many of the same people were here. No matter, he decided, he was here and here he would stay.

Sequoyah did not have as much trouble getting started as he might have thought. Merchandise had a way of traveling on the early frontier, and many of his fine silver pieces had appeared in shops in Willstown long before he reached there. Before long he was turning out more silver ornaments than ever before.

At the same time, Sequoyah turned to his new interest, blacksmithing. When he had saved up enough silver coins, he made the short trip to Willstown. He returned with hammers, forceps, and pliers of various sizes. The next day he went again to Willstown, this time to buy a supply of iron and steel. He made still another journey to purchase bricks with which to set up his forge. Then he made a goatskin bellows which he used to blow up the fire in the forge.

A cabin built by Sequoyah in Oklahoma later in his life, but probably similar to his home in Willstown

Now Sequoyah began to shoe horses and mend broken plows, hoes, and axes. He learned to sharpen tomahawks and fix the broken hammer of a musket. Women came to him with copper kettles that needed mending. Copper was harder for him to work with, but he eventually learned how to patch a copper pot by riveting a piece over the hole.

Sequoyah had not been in the Coosa village very long when he met and married Utiya, an Indian woman from a neighboring Cherokee town. After his marriage he continued to work as a blacksmith and occasionally found time to do a little silver work.

As the years passed, Sequoyah became the father of four boys, all of whom he was very proud. He supported his family well. His house was a model of neatness. His vegetable garden and flower beds were the envy of all others. The Lame One had come a long way. Other Cherokees respected him, and they seemed to have forgotten that they had made fun of him when he was a boy. He even had a voice on the tribal council.

But Sequoyah was worried. For a long time he had felt that something was missing from the Cherokee way of life. He first noticed it in the other villages he visited. The Principal People were slowly drifting apart. In his own village, too, he saw that contacts with the white man were affecting the Cherokee way of life more than ever.

There were those who followed and believed in the old ways, in the old spells and the old magic. There were those who hated the whites and wanted to be far from them, except when they had an opportunity to kill them. Some Cherokees were getting lazy and discontented, wanting always to be where they were not. There were others who carried the seeds of hatred, suspicion, and anger within themselves. And there were those who lacked wisdom and did not even desire it.

Saddest of all, Sequoyah thought, was that a great number of Cherokees were no longer interested in living as their fathers had done. Many had taken up the white man's ways and intended to continue. Others had become witless drunks from drinking the white man's whiskey.

Sequoyah was also worried about the white man. Time after time the white government had promised the Cherokees protected land. Yet more and more traders' licenses were being granted by the government to men who wanted to go into or through Indian country. More than once he had noticed that the roads and the rivers of the Cherokee Nation were becoming more heavily traveled by the white settlers from the east.

During this period, white Christian missionaries arrived to build schools and missions and teach the Indians who were sent to them for schooling. The missionaries hoped that once they had taught and converted the children, these children would, in time, teach and convert their parents. But the missionaries often overlooked the fact that the Indian children first had to learn to speak and understand the English language before they could use it in reading and writing. Consequently, not only did many dedicated missionaries get discouraged, but many children did also. As a result, by the early 1800s there were still only a few Indians who could read or write.

The day was approaching, however, when the Principal

People would not only be able to read and write, but would be able to read and write in their own language, in their own way.

As more years went by, Sequoyah grew more and more restless. For some reason he could not ignore the feeling that he was letting his people down. He knew they needed something to hold them together, because once an Indian left his family and his people's ways, he became a part of nothing.

The Lame One wanted desperately to help his people, but nothing he had done so far had helped them. For almost twenty-five years he had learned to use and to understand the white man's tools, yet he couldn't help but think that there was another tool, one more important than all the others, which would give the Cherokees the new wisdom and strength they so badly needed. Sequoyah did not have the least idea what that tool would be.

On a summer day in the Cherokee town of Sauta in the year 1809, he was going to discover the "tool," but it would be four years later before he fully understood its use.

CHAPTER IV

Beginning of a Miracle

Sequoyah was thirty-nine when he went to the Cherokee town of Sauta to do some blacksmithing for friends. It was his usual practice, after finishing a piece of which he was particularly proud, to light his long-stemmed clay pipe and either tell stories about the old times or discuss the problems of the day.

That particular day his friends had been talking of the wonderful and superior talents of the white people. One of his friends showed him a book that had been taken from a captured white man. Sequoyah looked at the book for a while, then asked, "Of what use is it?"

"It is filled with the white man's magic," said the friend, "magic that only another white man can understand."

The friend held the book high over his head, and as the wind blew through the pages, he added, "The medicine men say it is the talking leaves of the white man."

All agreed that it was a great wonder, and that it was indeed an art far beyond the reach of the Cherokee. All, that is, except The Lame One, who said firmly, "You are all fools. It requires no great brains or magic to make marks for talk. Why, the thing is very easy. I myself can do it."

Taking up a large stone he struck it with a piece of slate. After a few minutes he told them what he had written by making a different mark for each word.

The others laughed at him. "You are the one who is a fool, Sequoyah. If you had not told us what you put on the rock we would not know. How do you expect others to know what you mean? With the white man's talk, all who see it can understand."

Some of the watchers laughed again, shrugged their shoulders, and walked away. The few who stayed let the matter drop. Sequoyah did not think it funny, for something had happened inside of him. He did not quite understand the feeling, but it was like being in a darkened room that suddenly filled with light, only to have the light go out again. It was a feeling he had never before experienced, and one that Sequoyah knew would require much thought.

During the next three years, the memory of what had happened that day in Sauta only teased Sequoyah's mind, because, for the most part, he stayed so busy that he scarcely had enough time for anything except work.

The reason for the extra work was that talk of war was running through the different tribes that the Americans were going to fight the British. If this happened, the wise ones of the council said the Cherokees would fight on the side of the Americans, although not out of love for the United States. Partly, it was because their ancient enemies, the Creeks, had already allied themselves with the British; it was also because they hoped that if the Americans were victorious, they might receive new and better treaties.

Sequoyah did not think this would hold true. The Americans had shown they were no good at keeping promises. He knew, though, that regardless of the outcome, the Cherokees would need more tomahawks, spears, and knives, and there would be many muskets to fix. He knew too that many of the warriors would want silver breastplates, armbands, and other silver ornaments to wear into battle. All this meant spending many hours at his forge, with little time for anything else other than keeping up his farm chores.

When the War of 1812 began, Sequoyah did not pay much attention at first. He had done his part; the weapons were ready, and the silver decorations were made. Besides, another child had been born into his house, and that meant still more work at the forge.

It was said that of all his five children, the last, a daughter, looked most like him. Sequoyah and Utiya had always wanted a daughter. Because her birth brought much happiness to them, Sequoyah named her Ah-yoka, which in Cherokee means "She Brought It."

As Sequoyah saw more and more of his friends going to join the white troops in Georgia, he decided that he, too, should join up. Up to this time he had never gone with the others on their raids to the white settlements, so in one sense of the word he was not a fighter. Yet without realizing it, he had been fighting ignorance all his life, with his hardest fight still to come.

Right now, however, Sequoyah felt that here was a chance for him to prove that he was as much Cherokee as anyone. So along with his good friends Archibald Campbell, Going Back, his cousin George Lowrey, and several others, The Lame One enlisted on the side of the United States at Turkeytown on October 17, 1813, under the name of George Guess.

It is hard to believe that a cripple would have been accepted into the army. For that reason there are those who say he was wounded in the service. Records in the war department, however, contradict such a theory. Therefore, it must be assumed that he was lame from early childhood.

Sequoyah served as a private in the company of Mounted and Foot Cherokees, commanded by a Cherokee, Captain John McLamore, until his discharge three months later on January 6, 1814.

Three weeks later, he reenlisted. On March 27, 1814 he took part in the famous Battle of Horseshoe Bend under General Andrew Jackson, whom the white soldiers called Old Hickory because they said he was fashioned from the toughest kind of wood. The Cherokees, however, renamed him "The Pointed Arrow," for where the danger was greatest, General Jackson was bound and determined to go.

Fifteen days after the Battle of Horseshoe Bend, when the war was practically over, Sequoyah was discharged at Hillabee, Georgia. When he returned home from fighting, not only his habits but his whole way of life had changed completely. Where once he had supported the family so well, Utiya now saw her husband becoming a dreamer. His vegetable garden, so carefully tended and productive before, began to show signs of neglect.

He no longer cared to work at his blacksmith trade, or to make the fine silver pieces of which he had always been so proud. Instead, he talked only of one thing. Sequoyah, The Lame One, had come home listening to the white man's "talking leaves."

No doubt the wonderful talking leaves had first whispered to him many, many years before in the Overhill country. But in the clouded imagination of the lonesome, crippled, half-breed boy, he had tossed aside the white man's talk of paper as just another one of their powerful medicines, like the magic of guns.

Then that day in Sauta, the spark had been ignited, and the war had only served to kindle the flame. Thrown into closer contact with the whites than he had been previously, he must have studied them with care. On more than one occasion, he must have seen the soldiers, huddled together around the campfires at night, feverishly making the mysterious dark marks on thin material that was no thicker than a leaf. Sometimes the white leaves would whirl away in the wind. They were sent away and talked of homesick husbands and fathers. And other leaves came back, and Sequoyah watched the faces of the soldiers as they read the leaves that brought news of wives and children waiting at home. For Sequoyah and the other Cherokees there had been no news. Some of them had not had one word from home in over two years. And Sequoyah knew why; none of the Cherokees knew the secret of the mystical talking leaves.

Sequoyah realized it was a great and important task that lay before him. He would learn the secret and then use it to invent and perfect a writing system for the

Cherokees. It would be such a glorious gift to his people, the best he could ever give them.

When Sequoyah told others of his idea they were quick to discourage him. Impossible, some told him. Sequoyah was ignorant, others declared. What no one knew then, least of all Sequoyah, was that in his ignorance would lie his strength.

Sequoyah still could not read, write, or speak English, so he began to attend the Moravian Mission School at Spring Place, Georgia. Even though he was too old to be a regular pupil, he would prowl about the classroom, peering over shoulders into the mysterious book of the white men. No doubt he was hoping for some clue to the mystery.

Sequoyah found that the talking leaves in use at the school were of no value to him. Even an English spelling book, given him to quiet his everlasting questions, was of no benefit, since it could be applied only to the white man's language. Once someone suggested that he learn English, but this was not what he wanted. He had to find a way to write in his own tongue.

By this time the idea of "talking leaves" for the benefit of his own people had taken firm possession of him. Already more and more Cherokees were breaking with their tribe, and some of them were starting to wander westward into the Arkansas territory. The Cherokee people first received permission to settle in Arkansas in 1782, when the land was still owned by Spain. After the year 1803, when Arkansas territory became a United States possession, more and more Cherokees went there to live. Soon they began calling themselves the Cherokee

Nation West, while those who remained behind were called the Cherokee Nation East.

Sequoyah was very concerned about this division of his people. He felt that if he could find a way to put the Cherokee language in writing, it would be a tool all Cherokees could use to "talk" across the miles, and this would help unify the now scattered Cherokees. With writing, his people could also set down the knowledge of the medicine men, and the records of the people could be kept forever. Only in this way could the red man be as strong in understanding as the white.

There must be a way to do this! But how? Where could he start? Others before him had tried and failed. Charles Hicks, another half-breed who once had been Sequoyah's friend in Tuskegee and who had become the first convert from that tribe, had spent several months transcribing the Lord's Prayer into Cherokee, using the English alphabet. But that was not enough.

Another missionary, Daniel S. Butrick, devoted several years to learning the Cherokee language, only to report sadly that he was not able to express himself so as to be understood by the Cherokees.

Their failures only made Sequoyah more determined to find a way. Given the proper incentive, no mountain is too high to climb, no current too swift to swim, and no goal too great to reach, if one were a Cherokee. And Sequoyah was a Cherokee. More than that, he was of the Red Paint Clan. Had Old Kaluna not said that it would be one of the Red Paint Clan who would help the Cherokees in their time of trouble?

His mind made up at last, Sequoyah became filled

with a sort of inner peace. Quietly, patiently, stubbornly, he persisted in his research. Finally, he decided that he would start by developing a form of picture writing. The pictures had talked for him in his drawings and on his silver pieces. Would they talk again? Perhaps they would!

For long hours he sat in the sunshine with charcoal and sycamore bark, drawing pictographs by the dozens. His idea was to draw a picture of every Cherokee word. But there were thousands of words in the Cherokee language, and every word had at least one idea behind it. After many months he found he was trying to capture whole thoughts in one picture, and their number and variety seemed endless. He saw that it would take a lifetime to memorize a picture for every word and thought in Cherokee, so this kind of writing system was simply not practical. Realizing that his first approach was hopeless, he gave it up.

A mountain, however, has more than one path to the top, so Sequoyah looked for another way. Caught up in his obsession, he withdrew further and further into his dream world. Sequoyah was grateful now for the lonely days he had spent in the forest as a boy, because they had taught him an extra keen sense of hearing. From the cries of wild animals, from the talents of the mimicking birds, and from the voices of his own children, he began to learn that all feelings and thoughts were conveyed by a continuous and varying pattern of distinct sounds. He may have even taken his own name apart and discovered it had three parts, or syllables, to it — Se-quo-yah. Each syllable was itself made up of a number of basic sounds. Listening to others around him, he quickly began picking apart other Cherokee words, making marks on pieces of bark for each different sound he encountered. When he was with friends he became an eager listener.

If he heard a word that he could not immediately identify, he would interrupt the conversation and search through the piles of bark for the mark which stood for that word. If he could not find the word, he would grab his charcoal and a piece of bark and completely lose himself in thinking how best to represent the sounds in that particular word.

No wonder, then, that some of the Cherokees began to look upon him as someone crazy. After all, was not Sequoyah of the Red Paint Clan? Had he not spent much time with the medicine men and learned all their magic formulas? Cherokees who once were friends now whispered that The Lame One was making a fool of himself.

One of his closest friends tried to reason with him on this matter. "Maybe I am a fool," Sequoyah replied politely, "but what I am doing will not make fools of the Cherokees. Look, I will explain it to you. A word is nothing more than a wild animal. White men have learned to catch these animals and tame them and put them to work on material they call paper. That is the secret of the white man's strong medicine. I, too, will put words to work. When I do, the Cherokees' medicine will be as strong as the whites'."

The Cherokees were far from being ready for logical explanations about what he was doing. Sequoyah met only with blank stares and ridicule.

Still, he kept on with his work. He knew now that he was on the right track. He kept listening. He kept writing. He kept studying. His once cheerful, engaging face was now sober and preoccupied. His house fell into disrepair, and the rows of corn and beans had to battle with weeds. More and more the members of his tribe said that he was not quite sane.

As time went on, neglect caused the roof of his house to leak, and wind blew through the cracks between the logs. But Sequoyah had no time for carpentry work. Now there were not enough hours in the day for him to work on his invention. For in a little while, he told himself, he would know the secret of the talking leaves.

Days, weeks, and months passed. Sequoyah grew gaunt and thin as he moved about in deep concentration, his tired eyes staring fixedly at the lips of the few people who still came to visit him. He was glad they did, even if the visits were becoming rarer, and even though most came only to taunt him. Each new sound he detected meant that he was getting closer to his goal. By now he had accumulated several hundred bits of sycamore bark, each one inscribed with a sound symbol.

One day, when Sequoyah was busy and refused to fix something, Utiya in a fit of rage threw the carefully hoarded bark into the fireplace. For a long time, Sequoyah stared unbelievingly at his wife. "Now I must do it again," he said quietly. Then, lifting his daughter into his arms, the dejected Sequoyah turned to the path that led into the woods. Laughed at by his friends, scorned and humiliated by his wife, he left the village without looking back.

Several miles away stood an old run-down cabin that had been abandoned for years. It was there that Sequoyah started once again on his tedious work. Some say this was the turning point for him. For near the cabin, Ah-yoka, who was about six years old, spied a strange, flat thing lying half-hidden in the grass. Excitedly she scurried to her father and held it before him questioningly. Sequoyah was overwhelmed. Ah-yoka had found the talking leaves of the white man. He had seen a book like that before in the mission school. At the time he had thought the book was of no use. Now he was not so sure.

Examining the book carefully, Sequoyah learned that it contained twenty-six signs repeated over and over. This observation turned out to be the key that unlocked the puzzle he had been working on for so long. After studying the spelling book for hours, Sequoyah fell into a sleep filled with visions of a plan for the pattern of a Cherokee writing system that was years later to make him famous.

The work started once again from the beginning. This time, however, it was with a new direction. And it was easier — much, much easier. He realized now that, although the number of words in Cherokee was endless, the number of sounds was not. If he could just identify the sounds, and choose a symbol, or character, for each one, then the characters could be written in different combinations to make the words. Using the letters from the white man's book for some of his characters and making up others of his own, it was only a matter of months before a Cherokee *syllabary* (a set of symbols used to represent the sounds of different syllables) began to emerge.

On into the night Sequoyah worked, until early in the morning when he finally set down some of his thoughts. And Ah-yoka, quick of mind and eager to learn, traced her childish finger over the symbols and read back to her father what he had written. He had succeeded. The syllabary worked! One can only imagine the pleasure that must have filled his great mind and heart that day.

But his work was not over yet because the Cherokees still viewed him with suspicion. Dark talk ran through his tribesmen that The Lame One was in league with the medicine of the evil spirits. They were fully convinced that he was making black magic in his cabin. If a cow died unexpectedly, or hail cut down the young corn, or a baby died for no apparent reason, more likely than not the witchcraft of the Red Paint Man, Sequoyah, had something to do with it.

So one night, in an effort to destroy the evil which hovered over his home and engulfed the crazed Lame One and his strange daughter, Sequoyah's cabin was burned to the ground. And with it, up in smoke, went his new syllabary, which at the time consisted of characters for about two hundred syllables.

He had been forty-three when he began serious work on his project. Now he was nearly fifty. The great and humble man thought about all this and came to a grave decision. Right from the start his people had never understood his work. Yet to do this, after years of work, was more than he could take. He must leave this place where he was scorned and rejected. He would go to

*The Cherokee Syllabary
handwritten and as it was printed*

the Arkansas country where other Cherokees had gone. Maybe there they would listen to him. Perhaps that was the place to get another fresh start.

Sequoyah packed only a few possessions: his precious symbols, which he had redrawn on a piece of old deerskin, a hammer, a pair of pliers, and a few scraps of metal to support them on their journey. Then he took Ah-yoka by the hand, and together the pair made their way slowly out of the Smokies toward the Mississippi.

CHAPTER V

A Dream Come True

The two companions worked their way to the mouth of the Arkansas River where they joined up with other Cherokees moving westward. Among them was a widow and her eight-year-old son. By the time the group reached Fort Smith, Arkansas, Sequoyah had remarried. He found in Sally, his new wife, all the compassion, understanding, and companionship he had never experienced with Utiya.

From Fort Smith, Sequoyah and his family traveled to nearby Polk County, where he built his first cabin in the wilderness of the Cherokee Nation West.

Sequoyah spent the next three years tending his first farm, where he grew beans, squash, corn, other vegetables, and of course, flowers. In time he added cattle, some oxen, and pigs.

Sometimes Sequoyah loaded the family into an old cart, yoked up the oxen, filled it with tools, camping equipment, and food, and headed north through the woods about a dozen miles to a large salt lick which was owned by the Cherokee Nation West. Here they would remain for weeks at a time making salt.

First, drawing water out of the spring into a great

kettle, they boiled it until the water evaporated. Then, scooping out the salt deposit, they began all over again. Farming and making salt required a lot of work. Nevertheless, Sequoyah was never so busy that he did not have time to spend on perfecting his syllabary. By this time he had cut it down to about one hundred syllables, but that was still not good enough. He wanted to make his syllabary as simple and effective as he could.

Since his marriage, Sequoyah and Ah-yoka, who was almost as adept at its use as her father, had taught the syllabary to Sally and her son until they, too, had mastered it. Using the white man's paper, a goose quill, and a bottle of ink made by boiling oak galls and iron filings together in spring water, the family would spend their evenings testing and working with it. Sometimes Sequoyah would go out of the room and Sally would dictate a message to one of the children. Then he would return, read the sentence aloud, and send one of the others out of the room. Often they would make deliberate mistakes, half in fun, half to see if they could really fool each other.

After months of working in this fashion, Sequoyah found that many of the sounds he had first identified as separate syllables were now becoming recognizable as combinations of syllables. He concentrated on these until he could break them down into the different syllables that made up the combinations.

More months of weeding out the combinations, testing, and retesting followed, until at the end of the three years he emerged with a final Cherokee syllabary of eighty-six characters. These included six open, continuous sounds,

Salt lick log for cattle,
a common mountain practice

or *vowels,* and twelve dividing sounds, or *consonants,* in various combinations. A syllabary is not quite the same as an alphabet. In a syllabary, a single character stands for a whole syllable, like *tun,* or *kah.* An alphabet would have two or three characters for each of these syllables.

$$\boldsymbol{\mathcal{J}} = \text{tun} \qquad \boldsymbol{\Lambda} = \text{kah}$$

Now that he had completed the finishing touches on his talking leaves, Sequoyah knew that it was time to present his gift to the Principal People. Some of his close friends had already admitted to him privately that there was a possibility that it just might work.

Sequoyah knew, however, that the Cherokee Nation West still looked to the Eastern Nation for guidance. And if his invention were to be accepted, it would first have to be accepted by those who had mocked him, laughed at him, and who had openly blamed him for their days of misfortune.

Leaving Sally and her son to care for the farm and salt lick, he and Ah-yoka traveled the long road that led to the Eastern Nation. As soon as they reached the homeland, Sequoyah went to see John Ross, once an old friend, and now chairman of the Cherokee tribal council.

Sequoyah, however, had been the object of ridicule for too long, so John Ross was not the least bit interested. Not at first, anyway, but the gifted inventor persisted until Ross finally agreed to give Sequoyah's idea a trial. The council was due to meet the next day. Ross said Sequoyah could show his so-called miracle to them at that time.

47 A DREAM COME TRUE

Standing before the members of the tribal council with their solemn, unconcerned faces, we can only guess at the apprehension in Sequoyah's mind that day. Ah-yoka, who now was ten years old, was to set down on paper the words which the council would dictate to her. Sequoyah would then read back what she had written. To insure an honest test, Sequoyah was ordered to leave the room. That way, said the council, this "magician" could not memorize the words.

It must have seemed like an eternity to the inventor who sat quietly waiting to be called forth to prove his work. At last the time came when the door opened and a hand beckoned. Quiet hung heavy in the stale air as Sequoyah breathed a prayer to Yo-he-Wah and slowly took the paper that was thrust before him. Skeptical, smirking faces turned to the lame half-breed as he glanced at the sheet of paper. Hesitating a moment, Sequoyah removed the spectacles that he now wore, and rubbed his eyes. When his vision cleared, Sequoyah replaced his spectacles and began to read. And with a voice that was certain and sure and as musical as the chickadee's singing, he read it all. It was done! He had proved that the leaves could be made to speak in the language of the Cherokees.

Not so! The members of the tribal council were still filled with doubt. They had come to see a witch burn, and they did not want to be fooled into thinking that the white leaves could be made to talk Cherokee. After all, was not The Lame One of the Red Paint Clan? Was he not able to look into his daughter's mind to read her thoughts? They wanted more proof, they said, but how could they obtain this all-important proof? Finally, John Ross hit upon the solution. They would simply reverse the procedure. This time the council would dictate the words to Sequoyah, and the girl would then read the words back — if she could. This time, the girl would be taken a few miles away from camp to insure against any more black magic.

Ross was more white than Indian by blood, and he had received an excellent education at Dartmouth College. He was reported to have been able to read and write in English, French, Spanish, Latin, and Greek, and, of course, could speak Cherokee. It was decided that he would do the dictating. People say that Ross tried to throw Sequoyah off the track many times in dictating, using words which he thought The Lame One would not know. At last the dictation was completed and Ah-yoka was summoned. Knowing how much it meant to him, Sequoyah wondered, would she panic? Had he, who worked for ten years on his idea, become confused and misinterpreted some of the meaning of Ross's words? He would know soon. Soon, all would know.

The proud man fixed his eyes on the daughter who meant so much to him and with whom he had shared so much. But she was Indian; her face told him nothing. Quietly and with trembling fingers little Ah-yoka took the paper. Speaking slowly and with great calm, but in a voice that was heard even in the most doubtful of minds, she read the scrawling letters of her father. Not once did her voice falter. She did not stop reading until she had read it completely, several times in fact. When she finished she handed the paper to Ross, went to her father, and together they started to walk away. It was done! Sequoyah could do no more. He could not make them believe in the talking leaves.

The tribal council was stunned and silent, but only for a moment. Then, babbling like small children with new toys, the entire council gathered around Sequoyah and the girl, exclaiming their joy and expressing their regrets for having ever doubted him. Sequoyah the wise one, the greatest of all Cherokees, was right. All along he had been right. Looking at the strange marks on the paper, they now demanded to know how to set down that which would say their names, and the names of their families and loved ones. In due time, Sequoyah told them, he would show them.

At the request of the council, Sequoyah stayed in the East for a year teaching all those who came to him to learn. Among one of the first who came was his own eldest son, Tessee, who was by now a father himself, which made Sequoyah a proud and happy grandfather.

Other Cherokees came to Sequoyah as students, then they went out to teach still others. Wherever the Cherokees went they told the people they met of Sequoyah's invention. Farmers worked at it while resting their horses from the plow. Women left their spinning wheels and looms, and children their play, to learn to read and write. And it did not take them long: although there were eighty-six characters compared to the twenty-six English letters, each character had only one sound so there was no confusion in learning it. Before long the marks of the syllabary appeared everywhere — written on paper, scratched on the sides of houses, on fence rails, and, as

Sequoyah himself had once done, on rocks and the bark of trees. Even in the dust of the roadside, marks of the syllabary drawn by eager young fingers could be found.

At the end of the year when Sequoyah and Ah-yoka left for the land across the Mississippi, his son Tessee and his family went with them. Sequoyah also carried a load of letters written by people in the Cherokee Nation East to their relatives and friends in the Nation West. As soon as he taught the westerners how to read and write, Sequoyah promised, they would reply on the talking leaves of the Cherokees.

As word of the effectiveness of Sequoyah's invention spread throughout the Eastern Nation, missionaries quickly saw the advantages of using it in their mission and educational work. The first report of this was in 1824 when a young Cherokee completed a translation into Cherokee of the Gospel of John. The new syllabary was used again in 1825 when David Brown, a full-blooded Cherokee preacher, translated the rest of the New Testament into Cherokee.

Another missionary, Samuel Austin Worcester, who was in charge of printing and book-making for the Cherokee Nation, saw the new syllabary and was greatly impressed by it. Worcester told Sequoyah that if books were to be printed in Cherokee, it was only fitting that they be printed in the Cherokee writing system.

Their first project was starting a Cherokee newspaper. As a result, Sequoyah, Worcester, and others began the *Cherokee Phoenix,* the first Indian newspaper in a native tongue to be published on the continent. The *Cherokee Phoenix* was a four-page paper edited by Elias Boudinot,

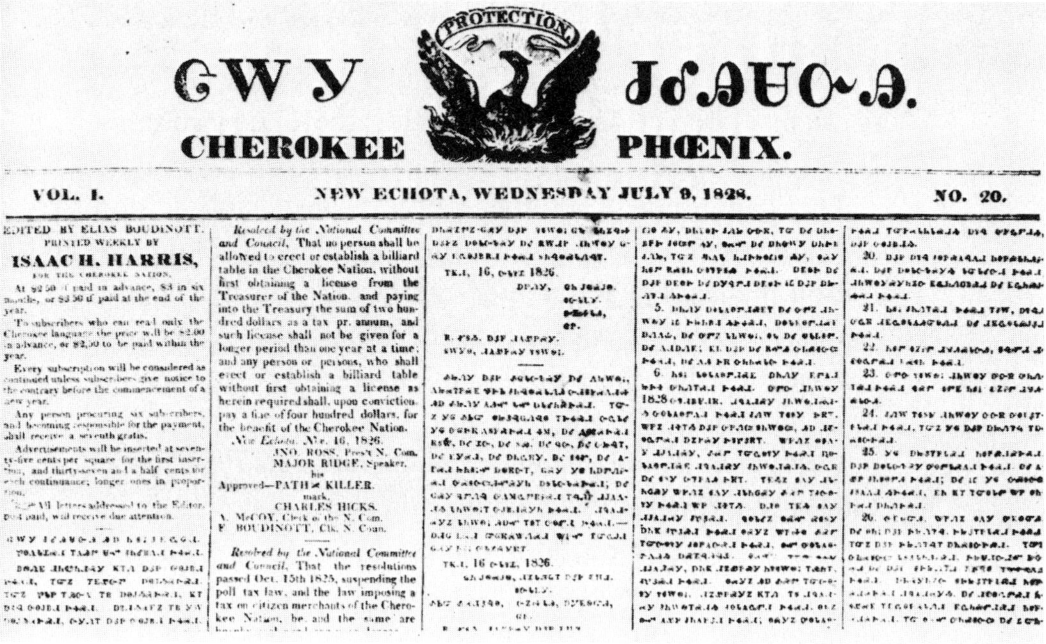

Masthead of the Phoenix

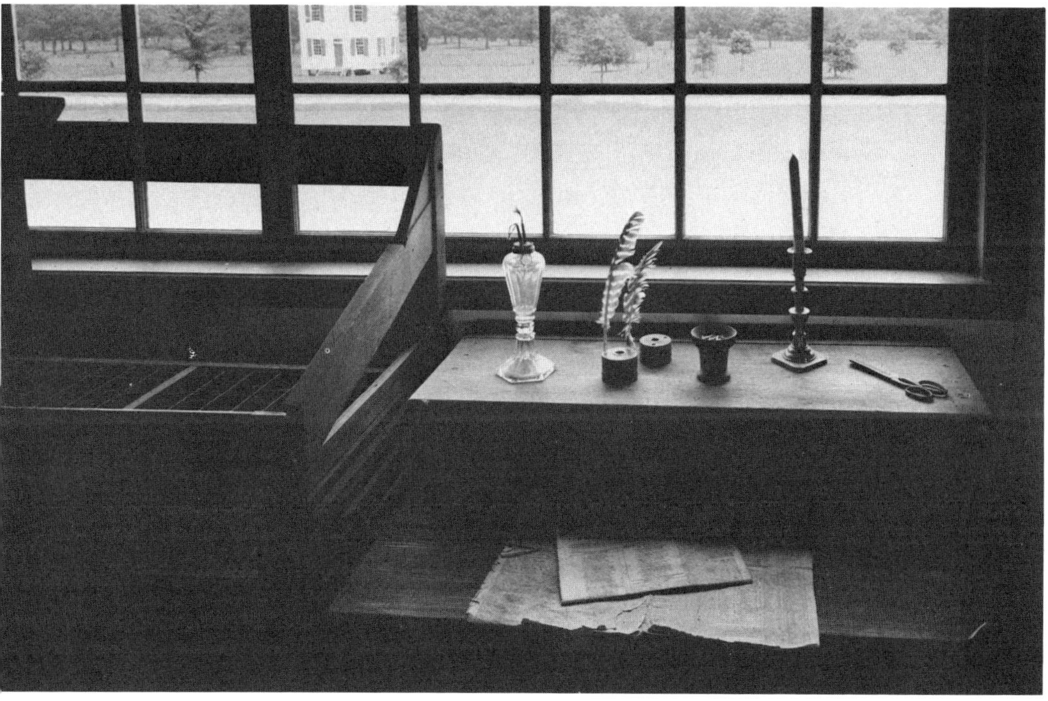

Interior of the restored print shop of the Cherokee Phoenix

a Cherokee who had been educated in Cornwall, Connecticut. It began publication in the Cherokee capital of New Echota, Georgia, on February 21, 1828.

The paper had a double purpose. Not only did it acquaint the Cherokees with the state of the Cherokee Nation, but it also acquainted the rest of the world with the Cherokees. Thus, part of the paper was in English and part in Cherokee. Subscriptions came in from as far away as Berlin, Germany. Often, the Cherokees sought out bilingual friends to interpret the information in the English columns. Consequently, the Cherokees kept informed on happenings in all parts of the world. In short, the *Cherokee Phoenix* offered the Indians many of the same advantages that the newspapers of today do. Other publications using Sequoyah's syllabary soon appeared, and it began to be taught and used in schools.

The only nearly complete file of the newspaper now in existence is in the British Museum in London. Some of the Cherokee printing type which was used in the Cherokee National Press is on exhibit in the United States National Museum in Washington, D.C.

When the first issue of the *Cherokee Phoenix* came off the press, Sequoyah was in Washington. He and six other delegates had gone there early in 1828 in an attempt to solve some of the difficulties the Nation West was having in the new land. The visit resulted in the delegates agreeing to exchange their land in Arkansas for a more spacious land tract farther west. At first the other Western Cherokees were bitter because they thought the delegates had betrayed them by letting the white government take advantage of them. As it turned out, however, the treaty did help put an end to the difficulties of the Western Nation. In 1829, along with twenty-five hundred other Cherokees, Sequoyah and his family left the Arkansas country and relocated in the new Indian territory in what now is Oklahoma, and which later became the permanent home of the Cherokee Nation. The home which he built near Sallisaw still stands, inside another building, and is maintained as a museum to his honor.

While in Washington the Cherokee delegation stayed at the Williamson Hotel where Sequoyah, who by now was a celebrity, was the object of much curiosity. Writers, scholars, lecturers, and many other distinguished people of that day sought him out. Among them was an artist named Charles Bird King who was well-known for his many Indian paintings. It was only natural that he asked to paint the portrait of a man who had accomplished so much. King's painting was the only portrait of this famous Indian painted from life.

Sequoyah made at least two trips to Washington on behalf of the Cherokee Nation. On one of his trips he was reported to have visited some of Nathaniel Gist's descendants in Kentucky, with the thought of looking up his white relatives. It is not known whether Sequoyah accepted these Gists as his relatives or not. But does it really matter who his father was? Greatness is born not of prominence or influence, but of a person's individual desire to succeed in reaching a goal or in fulfilling a dream.

And Sequoyah, The Lame One, had succeeded far beyond his own fondest dreams. The opportunity to serve so many has come to few men. Because of his invention, it is said that the Cherokee people learned how to read and write in a shorter span of time than any race, anywhere in the world. Within a year after the Cherokees had accepted Sequoyah's syllabary, they had passed from a state of having no written language at all to a high degree of literacy.

A lithograph copy from McKenney and Hall of Charles Bird King's portrait of Sequoyah

To understand how amazing his accomplishment was, one has to realize that this was but the sixth time in all of history that a totally new alphabet or syllabary had been devised. In addition, the invention of each previous alphabet had required centuries of study and experiment by many people, sometimes by many nations. Our own English alphabet, for example, came to us by way of Phoenicia, Egypt, Greece, and Europe, and it took centuries to perfect it.

Yet it took Sequoyah only a matter of ten years to create and perfect his syllabary. Besides that, we have the word of scientists and scholars that such a thing never happened at any other time in human history. He is the only person in the entire history of the world to invent, completely by himself, a simple and practical alphabet or syllabary. It was a tool so uncomplicated that there was not one thought that the Cherokees could not express by using it. There is no question about it; Sequoyah's syllabary was the work of genius.

When he returned to the West from teaching in the East, he was received with great honor. He had left an unknown and returned a hero. Never was an Indian so respected by his people. In gratitude for his supreme accomplishment and great gift, a gift they considered more valuable than gold, the Cherokees awarded him an income of five hundred dollars a year. This was the first literary prize ever awarded in the United States.

In 1824 the legislative council of the Cherokee Nation presented him with a large handsome silver medal which was inscribed on one side in both English and Cherokee: Presented to George Gist by the General Council of the

Cherokee Nation. Under the inscription were two crossed pipes which stood for the Eastern and Western Cherokees, and on the reverse side was a head meant to be the likeness of Sequoyah.

Accompanying the medal was a letter signed by John Ross, Head of the Tribal Council, George Lowrey, and Elijah Hicks, which in part stated, "The great good designed by the author of human existence in directing your genius in this happy discovery can not be fully estimated — it is incalculable."

In addition, the grateful Cherokees bestowed upon him the salt lick that he and his family had worked so faithfully while Sequoyah finished his syllabary. Yes, Sequoyah had come a long way from the once lonely boy who roamed the woods because he had not been good enough to play the Cherokee games.

He was, of course, proud of the gifts the Cherokees had given him. But what he wanted more than anything was to be accepted as a Cherokee. And of all his gifts, this was Sequoyah's greatest reward. Now, not only was he accepted as a Cherokee, but he had become, in one short year, a philosopher, professor, and one of the Advisors of the Nation — what the Cherokees called one of the Beloved Old Men. Now he was looked up to and respected and his wisdom was much sought after.

Soon, all his skill, patience, prestige, and his invention would be put to a critical test.

CHAPTER VI

The Last Farewell

When gold was discovered in Dahlonega, Georgia, in 1829, it was only a matter of months before some four thousand whites had crowded into the gold fields on land belonging to the Eastern Cherokees.

The white invasion disorganized the Cherokees more than anything that had ever happened before. Cornfields and gardens were trampled, fences were torn down, and livestock was butchered and left to rot right on the spot. As time went on the Indians found that the mountain roads were becoming barely passable for their buckboards because of the whites searching for gold.

Delegation after delegation of Cherokees went to Washington to protest their rights, but found that their pleas were ignored. By 1834 the plight of the Indians had only increased as more and more whites flooded into Indian country and found one means or another of getting Cherokee property into their own hands.

To make matters worse, the government of Georgia began to survey Cherokee land for distribution to the white newcomers. The Cherokees, said the government, were not capable of managing or caring for such rich lands, but this was only an excuse since it was the same land on which they had been living for centuries.

Bands of white soldiers were sent into the hills and valley towns with orders to tell the Cherokees to either get out or fight. To peaceful farm folks, who for three generations had given up the warpath except for lending aid to General Jackson during the War of 1812, it must have seemed a strange request. Resisting white men by force was something which only the oldest men could remember. Nevertheless, the Cherokees would not get out, and they knew better than to fight. And so on demand, they meekly surrendered their rifles and shotguns. When they asked for them back to use in hunting game, they were looked upon as hostile savages.

More delegates were sent to Washington, this time to talk to Andrew Jackson, who was now President. The Cherokees had their hopes cut short, because by then the white cry had gone up to move the Indians, who were regarded as "vermin," west of the Mississippi. President Jackson seemed to have forgotten that the Cherokees had once helped him win a war, and he refused to help them. Instead, he submitted to pressure and on May 23, 1836, signed papers calling for the Indians to evacuate their lands within two years or suffer forcible removal. For his action in doing this, the Cherokees branded him a traitor, and with great hatred in their hearts they forever more called him "The Chicken Snake."

When Sequoyah heard of the white government's plan for the Indian Removal, he knew that Old Kaluna's prophecy had come true. Using his syllabary, he wrote to John Ross and other leaders in the Eastern Nation, telling them there was no use in their trying to continue in the East. If they did, he warned, their misery would only increase. For already the Choctaws, Chickasaws, Seminoles, and Creeks had been driven from their land, and the Cherokees were less than the wind that blew over the mountain peaks. If they stayed, he wrote, in the end all would be broken and destroyed. It would be better for the Cherokees to save themselves by joining their tribesmen in the Nation West. The Principal People had to be united.

As a result of his letter, about one thousand or more Eastern Cherokees voluntarily moved West. Thankfully, these few, plus about two thousand more that left a little later, were spared the sadness and humiliation that was to follow.

During the next two years, the remaining Cherokees made no effort to get their possessions ready for removal to the West. Instead, they went about their usual business. Those who still had homes replaced or repaired their fences and planted and harvested their crops. While they worked at their different chores, they watched quietly and rather curiously as the white soldiers constructed wooden stockades in different strategic points throughout Indian country. Although the Cherokees didn't know it, these stockades were intended for use as concentration camps during the roundup of the Cherokees.

The Cherokees continued to send delegates to Washington. Once a petition containing over sixteen thousand names of people living in the Cherokee Nation and asking for a postponement of Indian Removal was presented to white officials. It was ignored, as were all the other pleas.

Those missionaries who tried to help the Cherokees by

calling attention to their quick rise to literacy and civilization were called "Indian lovers." Consequently, many were sent to prison for one reason or another, mostly on false charges. One of these missionaries was Samuel Worcester, one of the founders of the *Cherokee Phoenix*.

Several courageous people suggested to the government that the Cherokees be allowed to become citizens of the state of Georgia, thereby giving them equal rights. This outraged most of the whites; needless to say, the request was flatly refused.

There were many other individuals who sympathized with the Indians and wanted them to receive justice, but they were powerless to stop what was bound to happen. For the destiny of the Eastern Cherokees had been written two years earlier. On May 23, 1838 — just as "The Chicken Snake" had promised — the roundup of Cherokees began.

At the beginning of the roundup there was much confusion and fear among the Cherokees. One bewildered deaf mute who turned right when told to turn left was shot and killed. Another Cherokee who dared to strike a white soldier for urging his wife along with a bayonet was handcuffed and given one hundred lashes. Many Cherokees who had been away returned to find ransacked empty cabins. Worse yet was the Cherokee man who came down from the hills from a hunting trip only to find his wife and family gone, and nothing to tell him what had happened except a howling dog.

Surprisingly, there were fewer such incidents as the days and weeks went by. This was partly because letters written in Cherokee were passed among the Indians,

61 THE LAST FAREWELL

urging them to stick together. It was said that when soldiers came battering at the doors, a Cherokee man would often take out a Bible printed in Sequoyah's priceless syllabary and read from it to his family as they were led away, leaving cows unmilked and chickens and hogs unfed. Many had looked over their shoulders as they had been driven from their homes and had seen white men taking or destroying what had been left. Graves had even been opened and the silver and gold ornaments had been stolen from the dead.

As more days and weeks passed, the stockade pens began to fill with Cherokees. There were some who managed to escape the troops by hiding in the brush and caves in the mountains. The descendants of these Cherokees still live in the Great Smokies in North Carolina, and their history is full of stories that tell of their feats of bravery and heroism.

In the fall of 1838 the roundup was completed, and one by one the parties of Cherokees set out for the new land. By then an estimated two thousand had already died in the stockades, either from starvation, disease, or suicide.

The course of the removal ran northwest across the Cumberland Plateau to Nashville, Tennessee, through Hopkinsville, Kentucky. Crossing the Ohio River at Golconda, Kentucky, they went west to Jonesville, Ohio, where they crossed the Mississippi. From there on it was a southwest course to the Oklahoma country.

The first group of Cherokees set out in September and the last in November. Observers in Tennessee, Kentucky, and Illinois who watched them go by said later that it was a sight which they would never forget; there seemed to be no end to the procession. Cavalcades of wagons, carryalls, horsemen, and plodding foot travelers stretched out for a mile at a time, and at night their camps were like small cities.

There were men and women so old and gnarled that they looked more like supernatural creatures than human beings. There were newborn babies who along with their mothers were too weak to travel, and were left by the

The Trail of Tears *by Robert Lindneux, original oil painting at Woolaroc Museum*

roadside, sometimes to die. There were the blind; there were the Cherokees who had to be carried on litters; and there were the mentally ill. One party left the Nation very late and winter caught them plodding up frozen roads, some of them barefoot, trying to get to the Mississippi before it became impassable. They were too late and had to wait two weeks to get across. At the end of the two weeks more than half of the party of Cherokees had died.

Before it was over, the look of death could be seen in many faces. But in spite of the fact that they were often driven like cattle and that they encountered disease, strange diets, starvation, and other crushing hardships, the Cherokee's will to survive kept them going. By the end of March, 1839, the last stragglers had arrived in the new land.

History books often refer to this period as the time of the Great Indian Removal. To the Cherokees, however, it was known then and is still known today as *nunna-da-ul-tsun-yi,* or "Trail Where They Cried." Out of the more than seventeen thousand that began the journey, over four thousand never lived to see their new home in the west; they lay instead in unmarked graves along the Trail of Tears.

When the balance of the tribe arrived in Oklahoma, opportunity to serve his countrymen beckoned to Sequoyah once again. The "Newcomers," as they were called, made up over two-thirds of the tribe. When they were asked by the "Old Settlers" (the ones who had come to Oklahoma earlier) to meet with them in council to help organize a new united government, they refused.

They were afraid, they said, that the Western Cherokees would try to dominate them. This angered the Western Cherokees, who in turn said that the Eastern Cherokees had come to make slaves of them. Tempers became short and old hostilities flared, but Sequoyah listened to both sides. And as he listened he sensed all the bewilderment, the fury, and the sadness that had been building up for a generation. He knew the Cherokees had suffered much, but to take their sufferings out on old friends and loved ones was not right. He had to find a way to bring them together.

For a while it looked as if the Cherokees were to remain apart forever, especially after weeks of trying to get both groups together failed. Finally, Sequoyah wrote a letter in the characters of his own syllabary to the leaders of both groups, urging them to come together in haste to talk matters over like friends and brothers. He was sure, Sequoyah wrote, that all things could be settled fairly if each side would give the other a chance. It was important to do this, he said, or the Principal People would scatter, drift, and die.

To this both parties agreed. With John Ross acting as spokesman for the "Newcomers" and with Sequoyah acting as spokesman of the "Old Settlers," the two Cherokee tribes came and talked over their differences. Thanks to Sequoyah and his talking leaves, the two Cherokee tribes were successfully reunited on July 12, 1839, under the title the "Cherokee Nation," but now a thousand miles west of their original home.

Now that the Principal People were a nation once again, life was very good for Sequoyah. He spent his days with his children and grandchildren working on his farm, or telling them stories, which he was especially fond of doing.

Every so often he would saddle a pony and ride off to the nearest post office to get copies of books or pamphlets printed in his syllabary. In years past he had spent many enjoyable hours reading the *Cherokee Phoenix*. Unfortunately, that newspaper had been seized and destroyed by the state government of Georgia shortly before the Trail of Tears.

Sequoyah knew how much the written word meant to the Cherokees, so after Samuel Worcester's release from prison, he convinced him of the need to establish a printing press in the Western Cherokee country. For several years afterwards Worcester supervised the printing of a remarkable output of literature for the Indians to read. Much of it was in the alphabet of The Lame One. The miracle of being able to read these publications and knowing that others could read them because of his invention never grew stale to Sequoyah.

Sequoyah was still a famous man even though it had been almost twenty years since his invention had become known. His name had appeared in papers all over the world, and his syllabary had been the subject of many lectures and news articles. Many distinguished people still came to visit and interview the "Cherokee Cadmus," a title that had been given him by other writers and poets while he was visiting in Washington.

This title was based on Greek mythology. Cadmus was a Phoenician prince who killed a dragon and sowed its teeth like seeds into the soil, from which sprang armed men who fought one another until all but five were slain. With these remaining men he founded the city of Thebes. According to Greek legend, Cadmus was supposed to have introduced the Phoenician alphabet into Greece, but only after he overcame much opposition. Later, of course, many people and many nations benefited from this alphabet.

Such was the Cherokee Cadmus, Sequoyah.

Following his success with the Cherokee syllabary, Sequoyah helped the Choctaws develop a written language. It is from this language that the term "O.K." is said to have had its origin. Evidently, the term was accepted as common usage after President Andrew Jackson approved some public documents with the letters "O.K." Jackson supposedly adopted this symbol as his official authorization, and he is said to have written in his own hand in Sumner County, Tennessee, the following court record: "I, Andrew Jackson, Esq. proved a bill of sale from Hugh McGary to Gaspar Mansker, for a negro man, which is O.K."

Now Sequoyah seemed to have more free time than ever before, and he began to think about another idea which had always been in the back of his mind. Perhaps it was the impact of being in the Oklahoma country where dozens of Indian tribes jostled one another. Perhaps it was the success he had had with the Choctaws that gave him the idea. In any case, the thought of working out a writing system all Indian tribes could use and understand — talking leaves which could be heard all over the land — was one that had long intrigued him.

Sequoyah was about seventy-one years old at the time,

and he realized that in a few years his life would be over. Nevertheless, he knew he must try, for the puzzle of words which had driven him all his life had taken hold of him again. He began a search for the key which could help him develop a basic Indian language.

Sequoyah used every opportunity that came his way to talk to Indians from the other tribes living in the Oklahoma Indian Territory. He talked to Kickapoos, Shawnees, Chippewas, Creeks, Chickasaws, and Seminoles. And each time he found a word in another language that was like a Cherokee word in sound or meaning, he made a note of it. He visited tribes living outside the Indian territory, too.

Sequoyah was sure that somewhere, many thousands of years before, all Indians everywhere must have spoken a single great language. As time went on he somehow felt himself drawn by the stories he remembered from his youth, stories that told about the time when the Principal People and all Indian tribes lived in a place called Mexico. Sequoyah remembered, also, the stories that Old Kaluna had told about the Cherokees who had become lost many centuries before in Mexico and whose descendants were still supposed to be living there. They were known as the Lost Tribe of Cherokees.

Each time Sequoyah retold the stories to his children and grandchildren, he became more aware that perhaps this land far to the south would be the place to search for the key to the Indian mother tongue.

Then one day, after Ah-yoka's little girl had been digging in a mound of earth, Sequoyah found fragments of painted Mexican pottery. On the pieces of pottery were painted the sun design, a sign the ancient Cherokees, the Tallegewi, had once used.

It was all the evidence Sequoyah needed. He would go to Mexico. In Mexico, he was convinced, he would find the answer among the Lost Tribe of Cherokees.

When Sequoyah told Sally of his plan, she did not try to stop him. Instead, she said she understood and knew why he needed to go. He had felt the call to reach out beyond the needs of his own people, to answer the needs of all Indian people.

So in the summer of 1842 The Lame One departed for Mexico with his son Tessee Guess, a Cherokee called The Worm, six others, and three pack horses.

As they traveled through the vast Southwest, Sequoyah stopped and visited with other Indians they met. He encountered many, for it was a time in history when numerous Indian tribes were wandering in lands far from their original homes. He talked with Kiowas, Commanches, Delawares, Apaches, Wichitas, Potawatomis, Ottawas, and Wyandots, and always he searched and listened for the words which might reveal the origin of his beloved Cherokee.

Twice Sequoyah became ill, but he refused to turn back. Each day, he said, brought them a little closer to the land beyond the Great River of the North of the Arms of God, which was what the Mexicans called the Rio Grande. Each day, he felt, the key to the mother tongue was getting closer.

For months the party traveled southward until they reached a place near Waco, Texas. There the party stopped; Sequoyah was tired. The journey had taken more out of him than he had expected. He had noticed that his crippled leg had become badly swollen, and he needed to rest. Telling the others of this, Sequoyah asked all but Tessee and The Worm to return home to the Oklahoma country.

After a few days, Sequoyah said he felt much better and that they must press on. And so with a sense of urgency driving him onward, The Lame One and his two companions continued on for perhaps another two weeks before finally crossing the Rio Grande somewhere near San Antonio, Texas. Once across the Rio Grande they journeyed for two or three days more before Sequoyah called a halt. His leg had become so badly swollen that it was now of no use to him.

The party learned from passing Caddo Indians that they were within a four-day journey from a Mexican Indian settlement. So Sequoyah sent Tessee and The Worm to the settlement to buy supplies and try to persuade some of the Mexican Indians to come back with them, while he waited and rested in a cave overlooking the river. He would write, Sequoyah told them, in his diary and in a manuscript on which he had been working for some time, a record of the history and legends of the Cherokee people.

Waiting in the cave for his companion's return, Sequoyah probably wondered if he would be able to understand the Mexican Indians. He probably told himself that he wanted only to hear them speak, then he would know.

But we do not know what he learned on his trip because when Tessee and The Worm returned about ten days later, Sequoyah was gone, as were his diary and manuscript. There had been a flood, that much they knew. After searching for him for several days, they found only a piece of paper, caught on a tree stump, which bore marks of Sequoyah's syllabary. Neither could read the marks. The water had blurred the letters together.

From what later scholars and scientists have learned, we know now that Sequoyah would not have found the tribal languages in Mexico to be related to the Cherokee. These same people say also that regardless of where Sequoyah might have gone he would have been disappointed, because the wide variety of Indian tongues are so complex and different that there probably wasn't a single original language common to all of them.

Yet, had Sequoyah been younger or had he had more time, who knows for certain what else he might have accomplished? Even if he had known what we know today, undoubtedly he would still have tried to develop a general Indian writing system, because others had once told him the same thing about his Cherokee syllabary — it couldn't be done.

Saddened at the loss of Sequoyah, Tessee and The Worm retraced their steps to the Oklahoma country to report his death to the rest of the Cherokee Nation.

When the Cherokees heard the sad news, there were many who refused to believe that their beloved Sequoyah was dead. For more than two years they waited, sure of his return. To them it was just not possible for him to be sleeping the sleep of death in some strange land, away from those who loved him so much.

When the first issue of their new newspaper, the *Cherokee Advocate,* came out on September 26, 1844,

*Oo-ne-leh's letter of May 15, 1845,
in which he tells of Sequoyah's death*

it was only natural that their thoughts turned to Sequoyah, and their worry for him increased. By this time rumors had drifted back into the Cherokee Nation that Sequoyah had been seen in Texas, living with the Comanches. Other reports said he had been seen in Mexico, and he was old, worn, and ragged. Reports came in from all over — Sequoyah had been here, Sequoyah had been seen there.

All this deeply disturbed his countrymen and made them most anxious to discover the whereabouts of their Beloved Old Man. They expressed their feeling to Indian Agent Pierce M. Butler, who on November 23, 1844, petitioned the Secretary of War for funds with which to finance a search for Sequoyah. On January 17, 1845, the Secretary of War authorized the Cherokees to spend two hundred dollars of tribal funds in order to find Sequoyah and bring him home.

After a search of some three months, several Cherokees, including Tessee Guess and The Worm, wrote a letter to Butler using the characters of Sequoyah's invention. They reported sadly that the Cherokee, George Guess (commonly called Sequoyah) of the Cherokee Nation, Oklahoma Indian Territory, departed from this world at the age of seventy-three in the town of San Fernando, Mexico, in the month of August, 1843. How he got to San Fernando, why he was there, and how long he had been there, no one knows. The life that had begun in mystery ended in mystery.

Today no stone marker rises over the grave of quiet, serene Sequoyah, for although his death was reported, his burial place was never found. It was his wish, said

The Sequoyah statue placed in Statuary Hall in 1907

the Mexican Indians; he had been a part of Nature and he had returned to Nature.

Nevertheless, he is honored far beyond his own tribe's gratitude, and his name will always be remembered. At the northern limits of the town of Calhoun, Georgia, stands a statue of Sequoyah. There is a mountain on the North Carolina-Tennessee border named after him. In Oklahoma, there is a county which bears his name, and the state itself was very nearly called Sequoyah. In the Library of Congress in Washington, D.C., are representations of the alphabet-makers of this world — the men who have contributed the most to perfecting written language. Among them is the Cherokee, Sequoyah. When Oklahoma became a state in 1907, the first statue they placed in Statuary Hall in the nation's Capitol was the likeness of this notable Indian.

But in keeping with the magnitude of his genius, perhaps the most enduring of his honors is the Sequoia National Park in California, established in 1890. Those monumental wonders of the world, the mighty redwoods, the majestic sequoias, were named for the famous Indian by botanist Stephen L. Endlicher in 1849. This honor is especially fitting and proper, for the sequoias are the oldest living trees in the country, the most nearly immortal. Stretching more than two hundred feet toward heaven, they are a lasting tribute to the wise and gentle Sequoyah and his gift of "talking leaves." So whenever a new star appears suddenly in the heavens with a tail streaming behind it, do not be alarmed, for the Cherokees say it is only The Lame One still searching for the key to the mother tongue.

THE AUTHOR

C. W. Campbell was born and raised in the the picturesque Shenandoah Valley of Virginia. Since 1967, he has lived in Great Falls, Montana. His enduring interest in the heritage of the United States is reflected in his articles on word origins and history, and his short stories. Mr. Campbell's articles and stories have appeared in many leading magazines, as well as literary and religious publications.

The photographs are reproduced through the courtesy of the Denver Public Library Western Collection, Georgia Historical Commission, Library of Congress, National Archives and Records Service, National Park Service, Oklahoma Historical Society, Smithsonian Institution National Anthropological Archives, Ouachita National Forest, and Woolaroc Museum.

OTHER BIOGRAPHIES
IN THIS SERIES ARE

Joseph Brant
Crazy Horse
Geronimo
Chief Joseph
King Philip
Osceola
Powhatan
Red Cloud
Chief Seattle
Sitting Bull
Tecumseh
William Warren
William Beltz
Robert Bennett
LaDonna Harris
Oscar Howe
William Keeler
Maria Martinez
Billy Mills
George Morrison
Michael Naranjo
Buffy Sainte-Marie
Maria Tallchief
James Thorpe
Pablita Velarde
Annie Wauneka